We Celebrate

Valentine's Day

Bobbie Kalman

Susan Hughes

Allan and Deborah Drew-Brook-Cormack

The Holidays & Festivals Series

Crabtree Publishing Company

The Holidays and Festivals Series
Created by Bobbie Kalman

For Muci

Writing team:
    Bobbie Kalman
    Susan Hughes

Illustrations:
    Pages 8-9, 12-13, 16-19, 24-25, 28-31, 40-45,
    48-49, 52-53, Allan and Deborah Drew-Brook-Cormack
    Pages 32-33, 36, Jeff Pykerman
    Pages 20-21, Lisa Smith
    Pages 4-7, 14-15, 26-27, 38-39, Barbara Di Lella
    Pages 11, 46-47, 50, 54-55, Brenda Clark
    Pages 22-23, 34, Maureen Shaughnessy
    © Crabtree Publishing Company

Editor-in-Chief:
    Bobbie Kalman

Editors:
    Susan Hughes
    Dan Liebman

Research:
    Kathleen Smith
    Catherine Cronin

Art direction and design:
    Elaine Macpherson Enterprises Limited

Cataloguing in Publication Data
Kalman, Bobbie, 1947-
    We celebrate Valentine's Day

(The Holidays and festivals series)
Includes index.
ISBN 0-86505-047-3 (bound)
ISBN 0-86505-057-0 (pbk.)

1. Saint Valentine's Day - Juvenile literature.
I. Hughes, Susan, 1960- . II. Drew-Brook-Cormack,
Allan. III. Drew-Brook-Cormack, Deborah.
IV. Title. V. Series.

GT4925.K34 1986   j394.2'683

350 Fifth Avenue
Suite 3308
New York, N.Y. 10118

102 Torbrick Road
Toronto, Ontario
Canada M4J 4Z5

Contents

A special day of love

Valentine's Day is a day to celebrate friendship and love. It is a time to give little gifts to special people. Make homemade Valentine cards for your family and friends. Share a story and a smile with someone you like. Surprise your parents and do a household job without being asked. Write a letter to your grandparents. If you have argued with a friend, Valentine's Day is a good time for making up.

There are many ways of celebrating this holiday of love. Won't you fly a Valentine's Day kite of friendship with us?

Lupercalia, an early Roman festival

How did Valentine's Day begin? Why is February 14 a special day of love and friendship? No one is really sure. Some people feel that Valentine's Day may have started as a spring festival. Two thousand years ago, a Roman spring festival called Lupercalia honored the god Lupercalia who watched over sheep and shepherds.

At this time, Rome was just a small village near a big forest. Many wolves lived in the forest. People were afraid that the wolves would eat their sheep. They prayed to Lupercalia to keep the sheep safe. As Rome grew into a big city, the wolves were no longer a problem. Still, people continued to celebrate the festival of Lupercalia.

6

Choosing a love for a year

On the eve of the festival of Lupercalia, the young people of Rome played a game. The names of the women were put into a big urn or vase. Each man drew out a name. The young woman whose name was picked was to be the friend or sweetheart of the young man who drew her name. The couple would remain friends for a whole year. Many close friendships began on February 14.

From then to now

In later years, the Lupercalia festival was also celebrated in other places. In England, it was called the Spring Festival. Eventually, February 14 became a day for remembering one special saint. Do you know which saint? Right! Saint Valentine.

Goobletootle swings with love

February 14 is a favorite day on planet Goobletootle.
Write a story about how all these creatures celebrate
Valentine's Day in their own special ways.

8

Saint Valentine's story

Let me introduce myself. My name is Valentine. I lived in Rome during the third century. That was long, long ago! At that time, Rome was ruled by an emperor named Claudius. I didn't like Emperor Claudius, and I wasn't the only one! A lot of other people shared my feelings.

Claudius wanted to have a big army. He expected men to volunteer to join. Many men just did not want to fight in wars. They did not want to leave their wives and families. As you might have guessed, not many men signed up. This made Claudius furious. So what happened? He had a crazy idea. He thought that if men were not married, they would not mind joining the army. So Claudius decided not to allow any more marriages. Young people thought his new law was cruel. I thought it was preposterous! I certainly wasn't going to support that law!

Did I mention that I was a priest? One of my favorite activities was to marry couples. Even after Emperor Claudius passed his law, I kept on performing marriage ceremonies — secretly, of course. It was really quite exciting. Imagine a small candlelit room with only the bride and groom and myself. We would whisper the words of the ceremony, listening all the while for the steps of soldiers.

One night, we did hear footsteps. It was scary! Thank goodness the couple I was marrying escaped in time. I was caught. (Not quite as light on my feet as I used to be, I guess.) I was thrown in jail and told that my punishment was death.

I tried to stay cheerful. And do you know what? Wonderful things happened. Many young people came to the jail to visit me. They threw flowers and notes up to my window. They wanted me to know that they, too, believed in love.

One of these young people was the daughter of the prison guard. Her father allowed her to visit me in my cell. Sometimes we would sit and talk for hours. She helped me to keep my spirits up. She agreed that I did the right thing by ignoring the Emperor and going ahead with the secret marriages. On the day I was to die, I left my friend a little note thanking her for her friendship and loyalty. I signed it, "Love from your Valentine."

I believe that note started the custom of exchanging love messages on Valentine's Day. It was written on the day I died, February 14, 269 A.D. Now, every year on this day, people remember me. But most importantly, they think about love and friendship. And when they think of Emperor Claudius, they remember how he tried to stand in the way of love, and they laugh — because they know that love can't be beaten!

A Valentine's Day banquet

Many hundreds of years ago in the Middle Ages, people loved to celebrate Valentine's Day. In Europe, celebrations were held on February 14. People played games and exchanged gifts. The highlight of the day was the huge evening feast.

A feast of love?

Marion entered the large hall at the home of the young Lord of Portshill. Love lanterns and boughs of greenery adorned every wall. Marion felt that she might soar right into the air with excitement!

Marion and the other young girls wrote their names on pieces of paper and placed them in a bowl. Then each boy drew out a name. Marion sighed as she saw that mean Sylvester Switch had drawn out her name. Oh, how could she be so unlucky! Sylvester said, "My valentine!" as he tugged hard on one of Marion's curls. Marion knew it would be hard not to let him spoil the feast!

Marion and Sylvester joined the other couples at the long wooden table in the center of the hall. They toasted Saint Valentine as the horns and drums began to play a lively tune.

What a meal!

Then it was time to eat! On the table there was a peacock that had been plucked, roasted, and then re-feathered. When the ball of cotton in the peacock's mouth was lit, the bird seemed to breathe fire! Roast beef, small partridges, stewed quail, apples, pears, and figs were heaped on the table. Some people called these dishes ''foods of love,'' but Marion certainly felt no love for Sylvester, especially after he had poured his drink on her head!

The desserts were fantastic! Because red is a Valentine's Day color, the guests were served small cakes covered with cherries, plums, and pomegranates. Marion also tasted a special Valentine's Day treat — plum shuttles. These were red and purple oval cakes as long as her finger. The cakes were shaped like shuttles, which were used by weavers to make cloth. People thought that the cakes helped to weave love into the cloth of life. Marion hoped Sylvester would never weave his way into her life!

Finally, the feast was over. Marion had enjoyed every tasty morsel. Not even Sylvester could spoil this wonderful Valentine's Day feast!

13

My heart begins to sing

Spring is on its way.
I can smell it in the air.
I can see it in the faces
Of people everywhere.

Spring is on its way.
I can feel it when I run.
It makes me skip, it makes me hop,
It makes me jump for fun.

Spring is on its way.
I can see it in the trees.
They are waving, they are swaying,
They are dancing in the breeze!

Spring is on its way
And my heart begins to sing.
It fills with love for all my friends,
For the world, for everything!

Love is in the air

The North American tradition of celebrating Valentine's Day started when the settlers began arriving in the New World. Valentine's Day came just when it seemed that cold February would never end. It brightened up the winter days and was a good excuse for visiting, for parties, and for thinking about love. The settlers looked forward to it with excitement.

Gifts of love

Before Valentine's Day arrived, young people and their parents were busy drawing and cutting out Valentine cards. They worked by candlelight in the evenings. They made gifts such as strings of hearts, scarves, and embroidered hearts. They even made the wrapping paper!

Then came the red-letter day. Parents and children exchanged gifts and cards. Excitement filled the air as neighbors and friends bundled up in warm clothes, delivered their valentines, and then rushed home, bursting with anticipation. Would they find something waiting for them when they returned home? Who would brave the cold winter day to bring a token of friendship?

17

Other days for romance

Valentine's Day was not the only time the settlers thought about love. Sundays were days when young people had a chance to meet one another. Each Sunday, they climbed into their carts or sleighs and traveled to church. After the church service, a young man might work up enough courage to ask a young woman if he could drive her home. It was fun for the couple to talk and watch the scenery go by at the same time!

Will you bee mine?

Many young women were not allowed to spend time alone with young men, so they attended bees. A bee was a group activity which combined work with fun. It was a way for young people to meet and talk with one another. Many bees included special customs that allowed romance to bloom. At a cornhusking bee, the man who found a colored ear of corn could kiss the woman next to him.

Whether the work was cornhusking, apple-peeling, quilting, threshing, or sugaring off, most of the bees ended with a festive meal and dancing. Teenagers could mingle as their parents kept an eye on them!

Let's stick together!

Saint Catherine's Day was a day set aside for fun and romance. On this day, November 25, the French settlers remembered Catherine, the patron saint of single women. Unmarried women invited unmarried men to their homes for taffy-pulling parties.

18

Together, they made, pulled, and tasted taffy. They talked, feasted, and played games. Often, a young person ended up becoming good friends with his or her taffy-pulling partner. Sometimes partners ended up getting married! Do you think that when the couple married, they promised to always "stick together?"

Have a taffy pull!

With the help of an adult or an older friend, make Pulling Taffy for a Saint Catherine's Day party! You will need:

500 mL (2 cups) brown sugar
125 mL (1/2 cup) water
5 mL (1 teaspoon) corn syrup
250 mL (1 cup) molasses
80 mL (1/3 cup) butter

Combine all ingredients in a pot. Boil until mixture foams, rises, and then thickens. Drop a spoonful into cold water. If taffy does not dissolve, it is done. Let taffy cool in pot for several minutes. Stir from time to time. Grease a cookie sheet and pour taffy onto it. Leave taffy to cool until stiff. Grease your hands with shortening and ask your friends to do the same. Twist and pull the taffy until it turns a blond color. Then cut it into small pieces and eat!

Find the hearts

Can you help Patty find the hearts?
How many can you count?

Answer: There are twenty-four hearts.

21

A heavenly story

The Chinese and Japanese have their own love legend. It is not about Saint Valentine but about two star gods who fell in love. Here is the story of the heavenly lovers.

Love among the stars

Once there was a bright star, known as the Herdsboy, who cared for the animals in the heavens. One day, he took his herd down to Earth to drink from the Earth's many rivers. Imagine his surprise when he saw the Weaver Princess swimming in one of the streams! She, too, was a star. She was taking a rest from her work of weaving clothes for the gods.

As soon as the young stars saw each other, they fell in love. They wandered through the green fields, singing songs and telling stories. They picked the ripe berries and waded in the streams. Before they knew it, three years had passed. (Time goes quickly when you're in love!)

One day, the Princess' father and the Herdsboy's mother appeared before them. "Both of you have neglected your duties," they said angrily. "There are no new clothes for the gods to wear, and the herd has wandered all over the heavens. This cannot continue."

The Herdsboy's mother took a silver hairpin from her hair. With it, she drew a line through the heavens. This line became a roaring river. If you look into the sky on a clear night, you can see it. We call it the Milky Way. The river passed between the Herdsboy and the Weaver Princess. "You must live on opposite sides of the river so you will continue to do your duties," the parents told their children. "But one night a year, on the seventh day of the seventh moon, you may cross over the river and meet."

Now, every year on this night, joyful birds fly up to the heavens to form a bridge so the Weaver Princess can cross the river. And every year on this night, if you look up at the sky, you can see the Herdsboy star (Altair) and the Weaver Princess star (Vega) cross in the heavens.

The Maiden's Festival

The Chinese have three different names for this celebration of the stars: The Maidens' Festival, The Seven Sisters' Festival, and The Double Seven Festival. During the festival, young girls pray to the star princess for protection until they reach the age of sixteen. In honor of the Weaver Princess, they have contests to see if they can thread needles by moonlight.

The festival of Tanabata

The Japanese share the legend of the Herdsboy and the Weaver Princess with the Chinese. They, too, have made the day when the stars meet into a time of great celebration. However, the Japanese celebrate this day with different customs.

In Japan, the star festival is called Tanabata. A long time ago, Japanese farmers offered food to the Herdsboy star on this day. They hoped the star would help them to have a good year of farming. The wives offered cloth to the Weaver Princess star. They asked her to help them become good weavers. Children wrote love poems with brushes dipped in ink. They asked the two stars to help them improve their writing skills.

Colors and lights

Today, people in the cities also celebrate Tanabata. It is a time to think of love. Young people parade through the streets carrying lanterns and colorful streamers. Some carry tall poles decorated with paper flowers, stars, and birds. Narrow strips of paper are attached to the poles and bigger ones hang across the streets. The streamers are a beautiful sight as they flutter in the wind. They remind people of the stars of the Milky Way.

Celebrating marriage

Young married couples place bamboo branches outside their homes. They write poems on paper and then cut the paper into shapes of fruits, cakes, and tiny kimonos. They hang the paper decorations and streamers on the bamboo branches. They hope that the wind will carry their poems and messages to the two stars.

People are happy that the stars who love each other so much are together in the sky. They want to share their own joy with the stars. Like Valentine's Day, Tanabata is a day to hope for, or to be thankful for, love.

25

The facts of love

Did you know that hundreds of years ago in England, many children dressed up as adults on Valentine's Day? They went singing from home to home. One verse they sang was:

Good morning to you, valentine;
Curl your locks as I do mine —
Two before and three behind.
Good morning to you, valentine.

Did you know that in Wales, wooden love spoons were carved and given as gifts on February 14? Hearts, keys, and keyholes were favorite decorations on the spoons. The decorations meant, "You unlock my heart!"

Do you know how the expression "wear your heart on your sleeve" first began? In the Middle Ages, young men and women drew names from a bowl to see who their valentines would be. They would wear these names on their sleeves for one week! To wear your heart on your sleeve now means that it is easy for other people to know how you are feeling.

Did you know that many people give candy to their sweethearts on Valentine's Day? Candy is sweet and so are sweethearts! In North America and Europe, chocolates are sold in fancy boxes shaped like hearts. Some boxes have flowers and ribbons on them.

Did you know that on Valentine's Day in some countries, a young woman may receive a gift of clothing from a young man? If she keeps the gift, it means she will marry him. What kind of clothing would you give to your friend on Valentine's Day?

Did you know that some people used to believe that if a woman saw a robin flying overhead on Valentine's Day, it meant she would marry a sailor? If she saw a sparrow, she would marry a poor man and be very happy. If she saw a goldfinch, she would marry a millionaire. What do you think of these beliefs?

Do you know what a love seat is? A love seat is a wide chair. It was first made to seat one woman and her wide dress! Later, the love seat or courting seat had two sections, often in an S-shape. In this way, a couple could sit together — but not too closely!

Do you know this popular Valentine rhyme?

Roses are red,
Violets are blue.
Sugar is sweet,
And so are you.

Valentine's Day symbols?

A symbol is something that stands for something else. Some symbols make us think of certain events. What do you think of when you see a cake with candles and fancy icing? Birthdays of course! A cake with candles is a symbol of birthdays.

Most symbols have been around for such a long time that they mean the same thing to most people. Look at the symbols on this page. Which ones stand for Valentine's Day? Explain why you have chosen these. What events do the other objects on this page symbolize? Turn the page to find the most common Valentine's Day symbols and discover how they came to be a part of Valentine's Day.

28

29

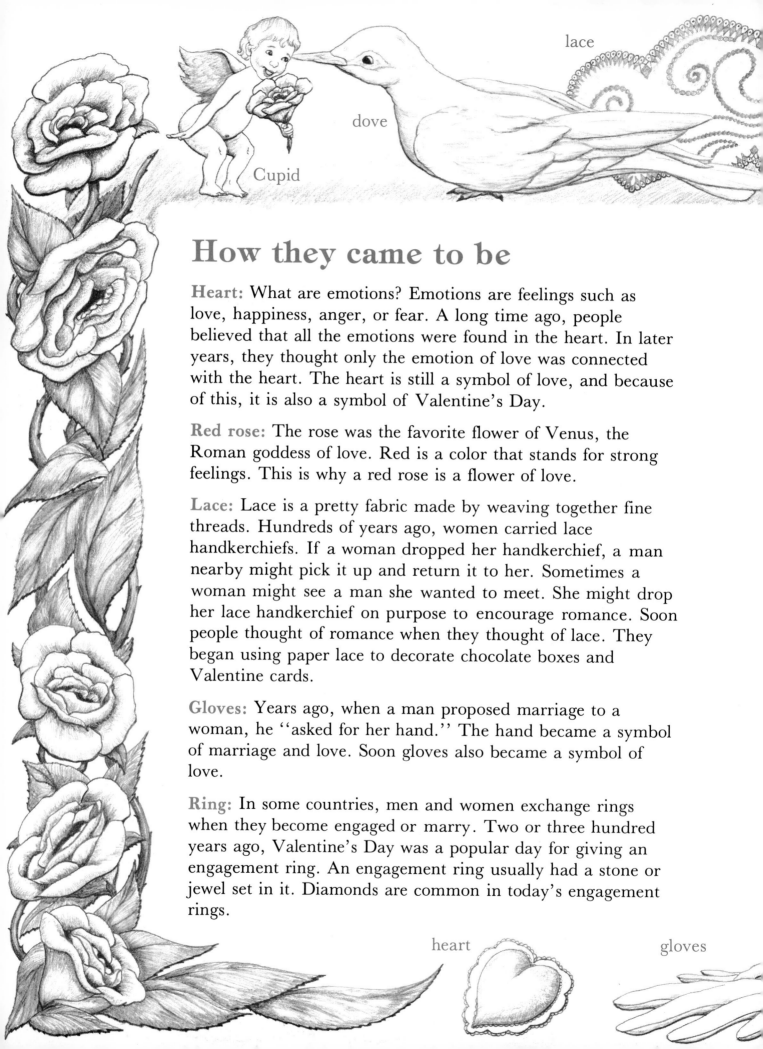

lace

dove

Cupid

How they came to be

Heart: What are emotions? Emotions are feelings such as love, happiness, anger, or fear. A long time ago, people believed that all the emotions were found in the heart. In later years, they thought only the emotion of love was connected with the heart. The heart is still a symbol of love, and because of this, it is also a symbol of Valentine's Day.

Red rose: The rose was the favorite flower of Venus, the Roman goddess of love. Red is a color that stands for strong feelings. This is why a red rose is a flower of love.

Lace: Lace is a pretty fabric made by weaving together fine threads. Hundreds of years ago, women carried lace handkerchiefs. If a woman dropped her handkerchief, a man nearby might pick it up and return it to her. Sometimes a woman might see a man she wanted to meet. She might drop her lace handkerchief on purpose to encourage romance. Soon people thought of romance when they thought of lace. They began using paper lace to decorate chocolate boxes and Valentine cards.

Gloves: Years ago, when a man proposed marriage to a woman, he ''asked for her hand.'' The hand became a symbol of marriage and love. Soon gloves also became a symbol of love.

Ring: In some countries, men and women exchange rings when they become engaged or marry. Two or three hundred years ago, Valentine's Day was a popular day for giving an engagement ring. An engagement ring usually had a stone or jewel set in it. Diamonds are common in today's engagement rings.

heart

gloves

lovebird

ring

Love knot: A love knot is a series of winding and interlacing loops with no beginning and no end. It is a symbol of endless love. People made love knots from ribbon or drew them on paper. Often, a message was written on the love knot. The message had no beginning or end. It could be repeated endlessly.

Lovebirds and doves: Lovebirds are colorful parrots found in Africa. Most have red bills. They are called lovebirds because they sit closely together in pairs.

Doves were thought to be favorite birds of Venus. They remain with the same mates all their lives. The males and females both care for their babies. Because these birds are symbols of loyalty and love, they are also symbols of Valentine's Day.

Cupid: Read the Roman myth on the following pages to discover why Cupid is a symbol of Valentine's Day.

Valentine words

Try to use these symbols in a Valentine's Day story. Are there other things that remind you of Valentine's Day? What are they? Make up your own Valentine's Day symbols. Use them in your story, too.

love knot

roses

Cupid and Psyche — a love story

Long ago, in a land far away, there lived a king and queen who had a
daughter named Psyche. She was kind and friendly and more beautiful
than anyone in the world. Venus, the goddess of beauty and love, was
jealous because everyone thought Psyche was even more beautiful than she.
She thought of a horrible plan. Cupid, her son, could cause people to fall
in love by piercing them with one of his magic arrows. Venus asked Cupid
to make Psyche fall in love with a monster! When Cupid saw the lovely
Psyche, he was so enchanted with her that he accidently pierced himself
with one of his arrows and fell in love with Psyche! Gods were not
supposed to fall in love with humans. What would happen now?

Soon after Cupid's secret visit, Psyche left home. She went to search for a
friend because she was lonely. The god of the wind carried Psyche into a
valley where there was a beautiful garden filled with flowers. In the garden
was a palace of marble. Psyche hoped she would find a friend there.

A promise of love

Psyche entered the palace. She could not see anyone, but she could hear voices! The voices were friendly. They told her not to be afraid. They said that she would meet a friend who would soon become her husband!

Psyche was very happy. She was taken to a wonderful room where invisible hands dressed her in silk and flowers. She was then led to a banquet room for a feast. Her favorite foods were served to her by invisible servants. Invisible musicians played the songs she loved best.

Can I trust you?

When Psyche went to her room that night, she was still sad. She had not met the promised friend. She felt even lonelier than she had before. Suddenly, there was a knock at her door. The door opened in the dark, then shut again. "Hello," said a voice. Psyche peered into the darkness. "Are you my new friend?" she asked. "I cannot see you. Shall I light a candle?"

"No," the voice said quickly. "You will never see me. If you agree to let me visit you every night in the dark, I will be your husband and best friend. I will love you dearly. But if you ever try to see me, I shall leave. Can I trust you?"

Psyche promised not to try to see her friend. Soon she was married and living happily in the palace with her new husband. But as time went by, she became curious to see what he looked like. One evening, when her husband was asleep, Psyche lit a candle. Who do you think she saw? She saw a beautiful, young man with curly blond hair. It was Cupid! Psyche cried out in surprise.

Cupid awoke immediately. "I must leave you," he said sadly. "I cannot trust you, so how can I love you?" Cupid flew away. The marvelous marble palace crumbled into dust around Psyche.

Thinking it over

Cupid returned to his mother's home. He thought about Psyche day and night. He knew that love must be based on trust, but he soon realized that Psyche had looked at him only because she was curious. Her mistake was, indeed, a small one. Cupid knew that love must also be based on forgiveness. He decided to return to Psyche and forgive her.

However, before Cupid could set off, Venus discovered that her son had secretly married a woman who was not a goddess. Venus was so angry that she threw her son into a dungeon! Cupid was overcome with grief. He thought that he would never see Psyche again.

In the meantime, Psyche did not stop loving her husband. She made a long journey to Venus' home to search for him. When Psyche asked to see Cupid, Venus laughed at her. She told Psyche that she would only free Cupid if Psyche would perform some difficult tasks. Venus believed that Psyche would soon give up and abandon her husband.

A happy ending

Psyche loved Cupid so much that she tried her best to complete all the impossible tasks. Finally, when Venus saw how strong Psyche's love was, she forgave the young couple. All the other gods and goddesses wanted to see them happy together as well. They gave Psyche a potion. When she drank it, she became a goddess. Cupid and Psyche lived very happily ever after, and to this day, Cupid helps other couples fall in love!

Valentine cards

The first Valentine cards were made in Europe over two hundred years ago. They were usually made from plain paper and were painted in pretty colors or cut into different shapes. Each card was different because each card was handmade.

Soon, English printers started printing fancy paper with hearts, roses, and pictures of Cupid. People wrote their Valentine messages on pieces of this paper and then sent them to their sweethearts. Before long, cards were being printed especially for Valentine's Day. The cards had symbols of love on the front. Trees, lovebirds, flowers, and pictures of Cupid were popular. On the inside of the folder there was space for the sender to write a special message or verse.

What shall I write?

Sometimes, the challenge of writing verses was too great for a lovesick man or woman. The solution was to buy a Valentine Writer. A Writer was a book of special verses written for different occasions. People looked through the book and chose the verses that best described how they felt. They copied the verses into Valentine cards and sent them to their sweethearts.

The Valentine boom!

Before long, valentines of many different shapes and sizes were printed with verses inside. The buyer had only to choose a card and sign his or her name. Big card companies began printing thousands of these valentines each year. Some cards were made of paper lace. Some valentines had seashells, beads, tinsel, fir cones, and feathers attached to them. Some were even mechanical. In Germany, mechanical automobile valentines showed passengers with Cupid as their driver!

Today's cards

Today, many people buy and send ready-made Valentine cards. However, the handmade card is still one of the favorite kinds of valentines to receive on February 14. Why? A person who takes the time to prepare a homemade card is showing the love that the words on a card can only tell of!

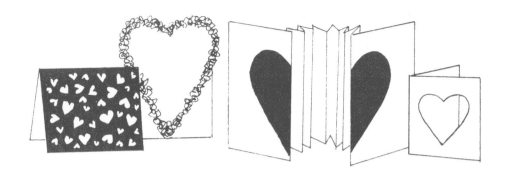

Make your own cards

Send homemade Valentine cards to your friends and family members. Maybe your teacher or the mail carrier would like one. Maybe your pet gerbil would like one, too!

Heart to heart

Anyone can make this simple Valentine card. Fold a square piece of pink or red construction paper in half. Draw half a heart on the paper, beginning and ending at the fold. Cut out the heart. Write a Valentine message on it.

Trim the heart with paper lace. If you do not have lace, use a pin or hole-puncher to make holes along the rim of the heart. Glue on sequins, tinsel, uncooked pasta shells, or anything else you can think of. Keep decorating your Valentine card until it looks just the way you want it to.

Guess who!

Make a valentine that really holds a surprise! Fold a piece of construction paper in half so that it forms a card. Draw a large heart on the front of the card, as shown in the diagram. Now, carefully cut along the dotted outline of the heart, leaving the outer edges attached. Do not cut along the solid lines. The heart can be opened up to form a window! Glue a photograph of yourself on the inside of the card. When the window is opened, your photo will be seen. Write a message that starts on the outside of the card and finishes on the inside, such as, "Guess who wants to be your valentine? Me!"

Pop goes the valentine

This is a very special kind of Valentine card! You will need paper, glue, and an empty matchbox. Cut a strip of paper that is as thin and twice as long as your middle finger. Cut a tiny heart out of another piece of paper and color it pink. Print on the heart in tiny letters: "Be mine." Glue this heart onto one end of the paper strip. Now fold the strip of paper back and forth several times so that it looks like an accordion. Take the end of the paper without the heart and paste it inside the matchbox. Press the strip of paper down and carefully slide the lid over the box. When your friend opens the box, your Valentine message will pop up!

A puzzling valentine

Make a Valentine puzzle card. Draw a huge heart on a heavy piece of cardboard or bristol board. Cut out the heart and write a Valentine message on it. Color the heart using crayons, felt markers, or paints. Use a pair of scissors to cut the board into many different shapes. (The smaller the shapes are, the harder it will be to put the puzzle together.)

Collect the pieces and put them into a bag or box. Wrap the bag or box in decorated paper. You might want to print on it: "I'm in pieces when I'm not with you." Another message might be: "Make my heart whole again." See if your friend can piece together your Valentine wishes.

Your very own creation

Use your imagination to create original valentines. Make them from paper doilies, crepe paper, tissue paper, or ribbon. Decorate your cards with cutouts from magazines or old greeting cards. Use scraps of cloth, yarn, aluminum foil, or cellophane. Experiment! You'll have fun creating something special for someone you love!

Valentine predictions

In the old days, young people did the things mentioned in this poem to try to discover who would be their valentines. Pamela decided to try to make a Valentine prediction using this old-fashioned method.

Who will be my valentine?

Who will be my valentine?
Who will be my love?
Will it be Luke or will it be Jeff?
I asked the stars above.

Two weeks ago I put Lad's Love
Into my pillowcase.
I knew that when I fell asleep
I would see my true love's face.

I tossed, I turned, I flopped about,
I said this rhyme times three:
"Saint Valentine, oh please be kind,
Let me my true love see."

The night was long. I tried my best,
But when the morning came,
I hadn't slept, I hadn't dreamed
Of anyone's face or name!

I want to know, I want to know
Who my valentine will be.
Will it be John, will it be Josh,
Or Mike, or Shiv, or Lee?

Valentine's Day will be here soon,
So I planted onions in a row.
I gave each one a boyfriend's face
And waited for them to grow.

The first onion that I saw sprout
Would reveal my true love's name.
But yesterday I found them gone —
The field mice were to blame!

I wanted to know who would be
my love,
But I've given up this game.
Now I know it's a lot less work
Just to try and guess his name!

Have a Valentine party

A wonderful way to let your friends and relatives know how much you care for them is to throw a Valentine's Day party. Start preparing for your party one or two weeks before the special day. You can make invitations and decorations, decide on games to play, and prepare delicious foods.

Invitations

Simple invitations can be made by cutting out construction-paper hearts, Cupids, and flowers. Make up funny invitation verses such as:

Roses are red,   Lovebirds twitter,
Violets are blue.   Turtledoves coo.
Come to my party.   Come to my party,
Yes, I mean YOU!   Or go to the zoo!

Write these verses on your handmade cards. Don't forget to add the date, time, and address of the party before you deliver your invitations.

Paper-flower decorations

Decorate your party room with streamers, balloons, hearts, Cupid cutouts, and paper chains. Did you know that red roses mean "I love you," yellow roses mean "I am jealous," and four-leaf clovers mean "Be my valentine?" Make paper flowers with different colors of tissue paper to tell your own Valentine's Day messages!

You need:
tissue paper (Valentine colors)
green pipe cleaners

Place five square (about 20 cm or 8 inches) pieces of colored tissue paper one on top of another. Fold them accordion-style. Wrap one end of a pipe cleaner around the middle of the accordion. The other end of the pipe cleaner will hang down. It will be the stem. Separate the tissue-paper layers and peel each one back carefully toward the center. Fluff them up until the flower looks full and pretty.

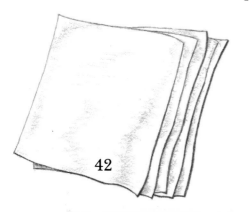

Clay decorations and gifts

Use Baker's Clay and a little imagination to make unusual gifts and decorations for your party.

You need:

500 mL (2 cups) flour
125 mL (1/2 cup) salt
185 mL (3/4 cup) water
shellac or three egg yolks, beaten

cookie sheet covered in foil
acrylic paints
colored string

Mix flour and salt in a bowl. Slowly add water, stirring with a fork and then mixing with your hands. Add more water if mixture feels too dry. Add more flour if it feels too sticky. Knead for about five minutes. Take a lump of the mixture and use your hands or a cookie cutter to mold it into a Valentine shape. For example, you can make a heart, flower, bird, or Cupid's arrow. If there is room, use the sharp end of a pencil to press a short message into the dough. Perhaps your message will say, BE MINE. Place the decoration pieces on a foil-covered cookie sheet. Using a pencil or straw, poke a hole near the top of each piece.

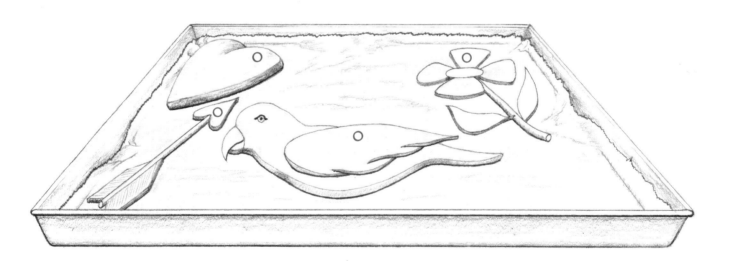

Ask an adult or older friend to help you use the oven. Bake the decorations at 180° C (350° F) for thirty minutes or until they are hard. Paint the decorations when they are cool. When the paint is dry, brush on a thin coat of shellac or egg yolk to give the decorations a pretty shine. Put a piece of colored string through each hole. Hang the decorations around your party room. Perhaps your guests might like to take a decoration home when the party is over. They can even hang the pretty Valentine plaques around their necks!

Valentine party games

Teach these "hearty" games to the guests at your Valentine party.

Mystery pairs

Long ago, young men chose their valentines by pulling their names out of a big urn or vase. You and your guests can choose your partners for this game in the same way. Half of your guests should write their names on slips of paper and put the slips into a hat or bowl. Each of the other guests now draws a name from the bowl. This will be the name of the guest's partner.

Choose one set of partners to be the first Mystery Pair. The Mystery Pair leaves the room and thinks of a famous couple they will pretend to be. They can choose couples from nursery rhymes, such as Jack and Jill. They can choose objects that belong together, such as a fork and spoon. They can be TV personalities or famous cartoon characters such as Mickey and Minnie Mouse.

When the Mystery Pair returns, the other players ask them questions to find out who they are. Everyone should take turns asking one question each. Questions might be: Are you TV characters? Are you people? Are you married? Only yes and no answers are allowed. The first pair to guess the identity of the Mystery Pair becomes the new Mystery Pair.

Bang, slap, clap, rap, beat

Beat, beat. Beat, beat. Can you hear your heart beat, beat? Play this game. It's really neat!

All the players sit in a big circle and quickly learn these five actions:

1. Knock on the floor twice and say bang, bang.
2. Slap your knees twice and say slap, slap.
3. Raise your hands above your head, clap your hands twice, and say clap, clap.
4. Touch your head twice and say rap, rap.
5. Tap your heart twice and say beat, beat.

Now everyone must do all five actions in the right order, saying the right words. Players who make a mistake are out. The last person left is the winner. If there is more than one winner at the end, begin again.

Watch where you sit!

Cut out large paper hearts. On each one, describe a silly or funny-looking action for the players to try, such as:

Make kissing noises.
Make goo-goo eyes at your neighbor.
Hop around on one leg and hug yourself.
Pretend you are a chicken flapping its wings.

Place chairs in a circle and put one heart underneath each chair. Choose a person to be "It." Blindfold that person and have him or her stand inside the circle of chairs. Everyone must march around the chairs until "It" says "Stop." Then the players each find a chair and sit down. "It" points to a player and then removes the blindfold so he or she can watch this player do the activity that is printed on the heart under his or her chair. The player then becomes "It" for the next round.

A Valentine party feast

You can make wonderful treats to serve at your Valentine's Day party. Try these foods of love! Remember to have an adult or older friend help you use the stove or oven.

Imitation peacock

At feasts in the Middle Ages, peacocks were plucked, cooked, and then served with their feathers put back on. You can serve this dish of chicken and fruity rice in the shape of a peacock.

You need:
250 mL (1 cup) orange juice
1 L (4 cups) water
500 mL (2 cups) uncooked
    long-grain rice
125 mL (1/2 cup) each of : raisins,
    chopped plums, maraschino
    cherries, and chopped, unpeeled
    red apples
large platter or tray
1 to 2 chicken drumsticks per guest
1 package of oven-bake chicken coating
aluminum foil
colored tissue paper
celery sticks

Fruity rice

Combine orange juice and water in a pot and bring to a boil. Add rice and raisins. Cook rice according to package directions. Mix plums, cherries, and apples into cooked rice. Heap warm rice into an oval-shaped mound on a platter or tray, as shown in the picture.

Drumsticks

Coat drumsticks with chicken coating. Bake in preheated oven at medium heat for 20 to 25 minutes. When drumsticks are cool, wrap the narrow ends in foil. Cut tissue paper into wide strips. Wrap the strips in layers around the foil-covered ends of the drumsticks. Using scissors, fray the ends of the tissue paper to look like feathers.

Put the largest drumstick aside. Arrange the others around the rice mound with the feathers pointing outward, as in the picture. These will form the peacock's feathery tail. Place the largest drumstick, with feathers pointing inward toward the rice, on the top right-hand side of the rice. This forms the peacock's head. Place two short celery sticks at the bottom of the rice. These are the peacock's legs.

Serve your peacock as your main party dish. This will be a Valentine feast your friends will always remember!

Plum shuttles

Long ago, people thought that eating plum shuttles helped to weave love into their lives. Treat your guests to this Valentine dessert of love. Your plum shuttles will look just like the shuttles that weavers used in the old days.

You need:
1 box of fruit turnovers (strawberry, cherry, or blueberry)

Unroll dough into its square sections. Shape squares into shuttle shapes by pinching ends firmly together. They will look like little canoes! Fill with fruit filling. Follow package directions for baking. Drip on the icing to resemble strands of wool.

Berry Banana Shakes

Here is a recipe for a tasty pink drink. Serve it for a quick treat.

You need:
2 bananas
500 mL (2 cups) milk
125 mL (1/2 cup) strawberries or raspberries

Mix all ingredients together in blender. Makes four servings.

48
D.B.C.

Is my valentine at the zoo?

Valentine, valentine, who will you be?
A yawning sloth that hangs from a tree, or a
Long-legged giraffe with big brown eyes,
Elusive elephant of enormous size,
Nattering parrot or yackety yak,
Thirsty camel with a hump on his back,
Itching monkey, bumbling old bear,
Nosy narwhale, or panda rare,
Earnest emu who cannot fly,
'Smallest chickadee in the sky, or

Dandy kangaroo who bounds so high?
All of these animals in the zoo
Yearn to be mine . . . but I'd rather have you!

Pierced by love

Venus and her son Cupid were floating over Earth on a cloud one
Valentine morning, just as Mr. Merchant's class was at recess. Linda and
Jordana were fighting over a skipping rope. Jason had just tripped Emma.
Erika was stealing Emmanuel's apple, and Gina was pushing Stan into the
mud. But that wasn't all! William was pulling one of Surina's braids. Kim
had just stepped on Julio's granola bar, and Samantha was yelling a nasty
rhyme at Amy.

50

Venus and Cupid continued to watch as, even after recess, the fighting continued in the classroom. Mr. Merchant tried to get the children to settle down, but it was impossible. Alan was ripping Michael's picture, and other students were scribbling all over one another's work.

"This classroom needs some of your famous love arrows," suggested Venus to Cupid. "I was just thinking the same thing," Cupid agreed.

The invisible Cupid flitted about the room and surveyed the situation. Cupid's very first invisible arrow found Jordana's heart. She was just going to tell Rick that his story was stupid, when out came, "That's the best story you've ever written, Rick." Rick could not believe his ears. He was just about to yank his story out of Jordana's hands when a love arrow found him as a target. "Why, thank you, Jordana!" he beamed. "Maybe you can draw a picture to go with it. You're so good at drawing." Then he scratched his head. Why had he said that?

Cupid's love arrows flew all over the classroom. The angry voices softened to a friendly chatter, and the students were giving one another hugs and pats on the back. None of the children could figure out why they were suddenly feeling so friendly!

At noon that day, Mr. Merchant's students shared the favorite parts of their lunches with the other children. They helped to clean the lunch room and picked up the litter in the school yard. They played with the younger children and joked with the older students. Soon everyone was so happy that even the teachers came out to the school yard to join in the fun!

The whole school felt the love and friendship of Valentine's Day. It spread from person to person, and everyone it touched passed on a little more to someone else.

"Another job well done," Venus winked at Cupid. Then she gave her son a great big Valentine's Day hug.

Friendship fun

Is your classroom always a friendly place? Do you sometimes have problems getting along with some of the other students? Do you and your classmates argue and hurt one another's feelings?

Mr. Merchant's classroom turned into a place of friendship, thanks to Cupid's arrows. You do not need Cupid's arrows and you don't have to wait until Valentine's Day to turn your world into a friendlier place. Try these friendship activities with other children on any day of the year!

The good-will train

With a group of your friends, draw a long train on a large piece of mural paper. This train will carry anything you want. It will travel all over the world. Draw objects, words, or actions that you want to share. On one train car, you might write words such as understanding, sharing, and cooperation. On other cars, you might draw pictures of food, clothing, or trees. Maybe your teacher or principal will help you to send your mural to a school in another country. Your mural could become a symbol of good will around the world.

Share the sunshine

Are you sometimes in a bad mood right from the time you wake up in the morning? You might argue with your father about what you should eat for breakfast. You might carry that fighting mood to school with you. You might go through the whole day being cranky with your friends, your classmates, and your teacher.

Your bad mood can spread quickly. Your teacher might snap at some students because you have made him or her angry. Your friends might grumble because the teacher is upset. They might be unfriendly to one another and to you! Everyone's day can become miserable.

You have the power to make people angry, but you also have the power to spread happiness! When you feel grumpy, find a quiet place to sit. Then, close your eyes for a few moments. Take a deep breath and relax. Imagine you are in a place that makes you happy. It might be a sunny beach or the top of a hill. Breathe in the fresh air. Let the sunshine warm your face and your heart. Imagine that you are sharing the sunshine with your friends. Now put some of the sunshine into your pocket.

Each time you feel grumpy, reach into your pocket and take out some sunshine. Let it make you feel good again. Help your friends to feel good, too. Give a compliment, share a book or a snack, or offer to help someone. Watch for the sunshine on the faces of others after each of your thoughtful acts.

Getting to know you

Ask your teacher if you can work on a project with a classmate whom you do not know very well. Treat this boy or girl as you would treat a close friend. Before too long, you will find that working on something together is a good start toward a new friendship. Spend recess or lunch with your new friend. Share your feelings about your families, school, or hobbies. Introduce your new friend to your close friends. Encourage your other friends to make some new friends, too.

Seeds of kindness

Get together with a group of friends or classmates. Sit in a circle and hold hands. Close your eyes. Pretend you are carrying bags filled with seeds of kindness. Pretend you are scattering the seeds of kindness everywhere you go. What will your seeds grow to be? Picture the results that kind thoughts, words, and actions can bring. Now open your eyes and draw the pictures you imagined. Share your pictures with your friends.

Choose an act of kindness you can do as a group. Perhaps you can collect some clothes or toys to give to a charity. You might help elderly neighbors. You could organize a committee to clean up your school.

Stick on a smile

When you see friends or classmates arguing or frowning, say the words, ''stick on a smile.'' Get some of your friends to say it, too. You will be surprised how quickly your little sentence will catch on. Stick with it, and you will see many more smiles around you!

Make every day a day of friendship.
Make every day your own special
Valentine's Day.

Index

23456789 BP Printed in Canada 54321098